Mrs May had a puppy.
It was called Sniff.

Sniff ran off.

Mrs May was upset.

Sniff was lost.

Biff and Chip looked.

They couldn't find Sniff.

Wilf and Wilma looked.

They couldn't find Sniff.

Mum and Dad looked.

They couldn't find Sniff.

Everyone looked.

Nobody could find Sniff.

Floppy looked for his bone.

Sniff was by the tree.

'What a clever dog!' said everyone.